The Golden Book of Whispering Poems

By Christine Thompson-Wells

We support Cancer and Diabetic Type One Research.
10% of our sales will help to find cures for these conditions

ISBN : 978-0-9873523-5-4

Copyright© 2014 MSI Australia
All rights reserved.
Published by Books For Reading On Line.Com., under license from MSI Ltd, Australia

BOOKS
FOR READING
ONLINE

Company Registration No: 642923859
New South Wales, Australia

See our website: *www.booksforreadingonline.com* Or contact by email: sales@booksforreadingonline.com or: admin@booksforreadingonline.com

Front & Back Covers and Copyright owned by MSI, Australia
MSI acknowledges the authors of the images used in this book.

Book One
First Edition

Welcome

Poems are an amazing way to make a complicated message easy to understand.

When I write complicated books, it's nice for my mind to have a short break and to write something that is more light-hearted and easier for my mind and senses to absorb. It's also nice, at times, to have a laugh at the things people do or say or indeed at my own folly from time-to-time.

This is where poems come into their own. Poems allow a short verse to be said and yet it can pack a 'powerful punch' in the meaning or interpretation of the words.

It was my own sad experience when one of the children was diagnosed with a severe health condition that my lost and forgotten talent of writing returned, and that has been such a blessing.

Once again, welcome to the Golden Book of Whispering Poems, Book One, First Edition.

There will be more books written in the future. For this first book, please enjoy.

Please don't forget, to really enjoy poetry, you need to be relaxed. Before attempting to read these poems, you may wish to relax with our Whispering Audio Poem books available at: www.booksforreadingonline.com

Christine

Poem Titles

Page

Flowers

Angels – The Children We Love

Australiana

Flowers

Through Summer Sun and Winter Rains

Through summer sun and winter rains,
gum flowers are alive again...!

From flowering bottle brush
to grasses thick and lush.....!

Kangaroo paw, velvet and magnificent...

Sunny and sheek....!

Hot pinks....!

Scented leaves, powerful shapes,
greens, soft whites and purple too.....!
Fiery reds and yellows
for you to see....

Wild bees and insects busy and free....

With sparkles and jewels, they tantalise the senses....!

And Sturt's desert pea, splendid ~ dressed in its black and red gown...

Wildflowers ~ magnificent and proud...

Fragile ~ porcelain petals

Wild colours galore....!
Gum nuts and mystery alive in the bush....!

Some pretty and strong ~ others so fragile.....
but the heart of a song.....

For you this is a memory to hold in your mind....

For every good memory is a treasure to have and to find...!

So hold your good memories close to your dreams....

Each good memory is a secret place to go when life seems unfair and it's difficult to know...

Just why things happen the way that they do...!

For life has its challenges' for you to go through...

But with a good memory of beauty you can see your way too,

and know that the love of the flower is standing by you...!

The Australian Bluebell
The Wahlenbergia

The Australian Bluebell grows where the
land, sky, and sunshine shows...

It's vivid blue petals with colour so
grand...

It's sure to be seen within the rocks and
the sand...

The colour is as blue the sky above and
shows its reflection with enduring love...

The tiny blue flowers are defined when in
their magnificent sew...

For out of the soil in the springtime they
fight for survival while they struggle to
grow...!

When the weather is kind, they make their appearance in the mountains of view...

And are there for us all with a blue so new...!

They last their life for a short time as they grow...!

There is nothing so wonderful in the time that they show...!

This tiny flower is humble so few, with each its own life to perfect

...and make as part of the new...!
For the beauty we behold in the honour of seeing...

Is by far a gift of nature and not for the fleeing...!

*So, take the time to wonder at the shape
and the form of this tiny arrival ~*

*For while its life is short-lived, it's our
pleasure to marvel...!*

*This tiny Bluebell has a name so splendid
~
A name far larger than the bloom when
ended...!*

*The tiny Bluebell is named Wahlenbergia
and is nature's perfect gift...*

*It exists for the making and is for the
viewing and not for taking...!*

*Just take the time to look, respect, and a
time to wonder...*

*For this tiny flower has its time for
survival...*

*And to make good for next year's
arrival...!*

Whispering Roses

Perfume and fragrance fill the air when you see a rose standing there...!

So pure and untouched...

Petals of velvets, satins. and silks...!

Kissed by the summer sunshine and blessed by the stars at night...

Scented and soft...

Red roses for the love of you...

A pink rose for the love of your heart...

A white rose for the love of your life... And a yellow rose for the love of your dreams...! Blossoms, buds and dreams ~

Roses ~ make your heart sing...

Friendship and love, and a whole lot more...!

A bunch of white roses and peace to restore...

And the centre of you...!

Fresh petals with raindrops...

A yearning for life...

To show the jewel of the flower they possess ~

Roses ~

Your love and your thoughts....

Diamonds and rubies cannot be compared...

For the beauty of a rose is soothing when shared...!

Mystical and loving and fleeting the senses...

The moment is captured, and the memory can linger...!

A rose is a flower that brings comfort to you when you are on your journey to see your dreams through...!

So, take the time to think, 'why these roses have the power to bring such peace and reflection to you....?'

Whispering Wildflowers
So Pure And Free

*So pure and free with petals of deep
purple
reflecting the sun...*

*Daisies and blue cornflowers,
how proudly they stand...*

*Flowers of sun-kissed yellow and
white of the snow...!*

...reds, blues and greens as they grow...!

Scented, soft their petals...

*Dew as fresh as a mountain
stream...*

*Pinks, purples and flowers of blue with
petals sending their signals of beauty to
you...!*

Fields of white daisies, sunshine, and raindrops for you to enjoy...

Wild life and bumble bees forage and seek...!

Through life's difficult times, nature's gifts' may seem humble and meek...!

Nature's offerings' in abundance and in the fields as they grow ~

Wildflowers...!

Bluebells, campion, stitchwart, and wild parsley show...!

Each brings its friendship for you to share...

Yellow cowslips and blue for-get-me-nots there...!

Wildflowers ~ their cost is free...

*Wild foxgloves in profusion ~ each flower
has its beauty for you to admire...!*

*Yellow daisies an exception ~ daffodils,
crisp and sharp...!*

*Wild roses with colours of mist and
spring showering rain...*

*With wildflowers and sparkles of dew ~
these heavenly gifts were created for
you...!*

*So, while the day is still yours ~ take the
time to think the gifts through...*

*With all that is said and the hurt you may
feel,
the thought of a flower has the power to
restore and to heal...!*

Whispering Lilies
With Colours Of Cheer

Whispering lilies with colours
of cheer...

Loving the moment and the
time that is here...!

Soft and gentle their petals, lovely to look
at ~

Handsome and strong...

Cool and reflective ~ loving and giving...

Some lost and alone, they yearn for the
sun...!

They give their love and friendship
as they grow...

Out of the still waters show...!

Lilies so pure and perfect of heart...
With petals of reflection...'

Lilies offer serenity, peace and love ~ the
sun is their joy with colours ablaze...

Or colours of the heavens
through the mist and the haze...!

The heart of the lily is perfect
with rare ~ its fragrance and perfume...

Captured just once ~ the time is not
forgotten...

For that time calls your name ~

Stop, listen and you will hear...

The rustle of petals as the fresh
breezes blow...!

The beauty of a lily cannot be measured
through feelings alone...

The love of a lily is a love of its own...!

When feeling alone and longing to know...

Life's outcomes and the way that you go...!

To reflect on the beauty a lily can show will allow you to see ~

Your possibilities and strengths are greater than you now know...!

Whispering Orchids

Orchids, pure and perfect...
With petals of a butterfly's wings...

and the lightness of a dancer's step...

A skirt of white lace...

And whispers of dew from the rain of the
night...

Beautiful flowers never to be seen
again...
Just look ~ gaze and stare...!
For one day ~ they will not be there...!

Perfect to see ~
white, gold, and transparent...

Colours of a morning sunrise...
Or a winter sky at evening time...

Majestic and majesty

They yearn to be seen...

Different shapes, colours ~
scented perfumes...!

Glitter, glamour, defiant with a voice to
be heard...!

Yet, light, and delicate and as free as a
bird...

As you care to see, an orchid is by far
both majestic and free...

Found in rocky gullies or by a mountain
stream...

Perfect in design ~ drawn by an artist's
pen...!

Orchids ~
It is with thought, love and concern...

The voice of the flower is needing to
yearn...

With sculpture of petals ~
Oh, so fine...

An orchid was created...
Take a moment and mellow the
thought...

The beauty, an orchid gives, is for you to
behold...!

And allows you to feel the warmth when
the world feels so cold...

Angels ~
The Children We Love

A Baby Boy
~ A Treasure We Have

A Baby Boy came into our world today....
he was just six hours old...!

We spoke, he listened ~

He turned his tiny head...!

Soft and delicate his baby skin...

With eyes of interest alive and within...!

The world is before him,
sparkling and new...!

A baby boy's interest is never too few...!

His time of growing takes on at great
pace...

*The world is adventure time with
learning to do...*

*In a baby boy's world, each second is
exciting and full of fun...!*

*A baby boy is a magnet for stairs to
master and climb...*

*~ the cupboards and fireplace are a
challenge to find...!*

*He's determined to conquer and learn...
all that life has for his young mind to
concern,
and for the challenges that yearn...!*

*A baby, boy is a master of disguise,
with a spirit of determination*

and willpower to see his life through...!

*To take the advantage to learn things
new...!*

*For every baby boy that is born,
each brings with him his light of the new
dawn...!*

*So be aware, the gift you have is for you
to nurture and love...!*

*Each time his clear eyes look at you,
know, that life is for living and seeing
things through...!*

*He will have his challenges in life as he
goes and needs you to support him*

through the highs and the lows...!

A baby boy is a treasure to hold...

So, know that life's gifts are fleeting,
but bold...!

A Baby Girl
~ She Brings Her Love...

Tiny toes and fingers she has,

with rose-bud lips and skin of satin and silk...

She sees the world from her tiny space...!

She looks at the faces, eager to see...

Tiny toes and fingers become a part of her fun

as she learns about her dad and her mum...!

The fingers she learns can be helpful when mum's back is turned and her makeup is near...

*It's ripe for the taking and smearing it
here...!*

*She learns about the flowers in the fields
and the birds in the sky...*

*She also discovers how life is a challenge
and learning is nigh...!*

*A baby girl brings her gifts and talents
too...!*

*Blessed is the moment she gives her first
smile to you...!*

*For a baby girl is a treasure and one of
life's precious gifts...*

*So, if you are a mum, dad, aunt or uncle
too...*

*Be aware, the moments you have
are fleeting and few...!*

With the baby girl's arrival and this gift for you ~ for time has a way of moving fast...

Life's special moments need to be treasured to make them last...!

Clear sparkling eyes and a mind ready to learn...!

Please take the time to admire and confirm...!

Tiny fingers are busy through life to affirm...!

How Precious This Gift...

For New Mums', And Dads'
Aunts and Uncles ~
Not Forgetting Nanna's, And Grandpa's,
And, Siblings Too...!

How precious this gift when a child is
born...!

A baby boy and baby girl is the gift made
for us to love and admire and cast a new
dawn...!

And yet, this gift is by far a creation so
great that little is known of the life's
journey this child may take...!

For this child needs the guidance for the
footsteps it sheds...!

The way ahead and yet gifted from above
is the responsibility that comes together
through unconditional love...!

The time will not stop for the actions you
take,
for little attention is given to the gifts in
the wake...!

A child's brain and mind is often
forgotten when we announce one day,

'That's your nose...!'

And as the child quickly learns and
grows...

There's a difference between their head
and their toes...!

One day, while nursing the baby to sleep,
you marvel at the miracle kept safe in
your keep...!

While your intentions are good and the child's safety you have...

For the child is born with technology advanced...

In its head there's a brain and a mind that cannot be chanced...!

It's now up to you, to take the responsibility too...!

A child has a mind that will see their life through...!

So, when you speak of the child's nose, eyes and mouth, please don't forget to go both to the north and south...!

The north is the crown of the head and south is the nose...

This is where the power of their brain and their mind actively grows...!

In the future, and when the child is aware...

Please respect this technology as all information is taken in and it shows...

All is at work between its crown and its nose...!

For a child's brain to create...

It needs guidance from you in all that you say and do and in all of the words that you state...!

By giving positive information to the child at the start...

This will eliminate hate and anger that may manifest in a young child's heart...!

Slipping Through The Net...
For the Children Who Struggle To Find Their Way Ahead...!

*Education is important and without it,
they are alone, and misled...!*

*For many the road to adulthood is hard
with nobody caring for the outcomes
they're fed...*

*With little guidance for the choices they
make...!*

*For some, the choices are limited with
little chance to a future that is desired
and for the most...!*

*Without the comfort of knowing that the
school days spent should be fun time of
creation and a succession to host...!*

But their everyday survival is hard for the most...!

They don't have the time to consider the talents they have...

Or develop the skills they need...

The skills needed in time to succeed...!

To slip through the net is easy to do, when a child feels unloved and the choices too few...!

We, the adults need to take care, to show that all children have the love that we share...!

For these children are the adults of tomorrow...

If we, the adults don't act today, we will contribute to their life of sorrow...!

So, take the time to reflect on the children we have, for all are as one under the sun...!

Without these young people, and some from afar...

We will be limited to reach full potential by far...!

It's time now to gather the children we have, for the time is short and there's no time to fret...

Without love and concerns, the children so precious, will slip through the net...!

Syrian Children
For Children Like Liliane...

The children of Syria no peace can they find...!

For the bombs keep dropping and their hell is confined...!

They face each day with hope and pray,

that this day will be better than in the past ~

For enough hurt and pain is held and will be there to last...!

Where they once played there were flowers in the valleys and birds in the sky ~ but these are now hell zones of blast...!

And no one is helping to stop the madness being dropped by the drones when they come in so fast...!

The hot sun is rising, and it should be time for school...

But mum says, 'stay at home today because I feel you are ill...!'

Mum's gentle words are protecting and comfort she knows that bad things can happen when the big bombs fall...!

Mum's words were right as she looked at the time...!

For the time was moving towards eleven o'clock...

The sounds in the sky were frightening she knew...!

That the bombs were close to the block...!

Many friends were no longer, and some were now refugees...

And some had seen the stars in the night sky for the last time they breathed...!

She wonders why this is happening and the anger is there...?

For she thinks,

'Life is for living and knowing you care...!'

Photograph, courtesy: A child carries a school bag near damaged buildings in Harasta, in the eastern Damascus suburb of Ghouta, Syria January 30, 2016. REUTERS/Bassam Khabieh

The Bully...
For The Children Who Have Suffered By The Acts Of A Bully

Bullying is a crime and a detestable act...!

A bully is one who intimidates, abuses another without concern and is aware of the fact...!

For a bully to abuse another child in the playground or while at home ~ such a cowardly deed should we not condone...!

And will continue if we don't intercede...!

For many, becoming a bully was not the intention at first to proceed...

The power of the action the bully gained was greater than anticipated and was difficult to refrain...!

Bullying became the habit and felt good when committed...!

Now is the time that the bully is fitted...!

For education the essence, and the way to go...!

Bullying is too much and we all should know...

Long-term hurt that is caused by the bully ~ this act is out for the throw...!

Going to school should be for learning and enjoying it so...!

So, all responsible people take note,

All children have the right to enjoy their journey of learning without any fear...

*And to enjoy their moments and the time
that is here...!*

Australiana

The Great Dividing Range

Blues, greys and greens as they show...

The Great Dividing Range where native trees grow...!

Snow gums, possums, and wildlife live where the mountain river of the Murrumbidgee flows...

To see the fiery range of the Snowy Mountains climb to ascending heights to meet the snow...!

It's the place where native mountain peppercorn plants sit and grow...!

Clouds and white clusters descending into stormy winter nights...

With blizzards and winds that freeze the winter snow...

But all is not lost when springtime arrives...

Gum trees, and wildflowers are eager to please, with new colours of spring they show...!

The mountains reveal the meaning of life and the purpose involved...

For life is about the love of the wild and the treasures the Great Dividing Range hold...

To see the Murrumbidgee with its gentle flow, and yet again,
the white-water tumbles to let us know...

The power it has when heavy rains fall,
it's strength yet again it has to show...!

*Magnificent and powerful, the Great
Dividing Range...*

Is splendid and strong...

*Grey gum trees are sprinkled with the
chorus of birds and the sounds of the
song...!*

*For life has much to offer when our
senses are free –*

*the sounds of the wild are heard and
resplendent for me...*

The days are as one:

The stillness of the mind is now...

The songs of the birds...

The water that flows...

The plants that grow...

And the animals that live
...are just some of the mysteries

And

Part of the throng...

Of the Great Dividing Range

...its voice and its song...

Hats

The Melbourne Cup...

Hats of colour in a flurry
with punters running and all in a hurry...

'Place your bets' the bookies shout...
'Time is short, and the race will be run...!'

Dresses of colour and top hats are
shining

The weather is fine with clouds and
punters looking for 'a silver lining...!'

They place their bets and the crowd is
silenced...

They wait – the horses are willing and
ready to run...!

The punters are out for a day of fun...

They gallop and work as hard as they can...!

The first bend is difficult to muster ~ but yes, they've all made it within a fine fluster...!

For some in the crowd, the excitement is brewing...

For others out there, their hearts are wooing...!

They know before the end of the race their bets are not worth the effort it takes...!

The men throw their hats into the air... ... the winners have won...!

The women have another fun day to share...!

The day is still young and there's lots more races to run...

*For some, the races are fun
A day to celebrate and wear a new dress...*

Walk in shoes that are too painful to stride...

With discomfort they try to desperately hide...!

The following day many heads are sore ~ a day at the races is the time no more...!

With the hats put away and now, only the memories left to share...

That's a time of fun and no time to care...!

Silhouettes
A Tribute To The Horse

In the mist and rain their silhouettes are seen again...

The wild stallion or the grazing mare, each has its life to live and its purpose there...!

The beauty of the face and the shape of the head...

The gate of the gallop, the sound of their hoofs...

It cannot be mistaken...!

The horse, a creature of beauty and outstanding strength ~

Is part of this land and the beauty we share...!

Through the summer heat and the winter chill
The horse survives and is with us still...!

Each, their personality ~

some friendly and soft, some bad tempered and angry for the days they fill...!

Each with its own longing to live the life they have within a field or the wild mountain range...!

The horse has the presence to make us stop...

This creature has mystic and wonder within its form and only allows us a glimpse of its beauty within the norm...!

To see such magnificence created by far, is a gift for reflection and one to admire...

In all that is said, and the stories told,
our love and delight for such...

It's silhouette, and beauty will never run
cold...

Sydney ~
An Australian Christmas
Through A Migrant's Eyes...!

Australia, this land of tantalizing beauty...

You've gripped my heart and I cannot let go....!

For the heat in the summer is by far so hot,
and the winters are as cold as the snow...!

The dust so fine and the flies are so many...

And yet we laugh as we try to eat our BBQ's with canny...!

I take a moment to paus and look at my meal and its covered with flies and yet just so many...!

Christmas is here and the feasting is merry, just wait a moment,

I think I must run, otherwise I'll be late for the ferry...!

The water of the Harbour is refreshing and pleasant...

and just what was needed after eating the over cooked pheasant...!

On arrival home, I look in the mirror and see a face that is red and hair that is dishevelled...

However, regardless of that, it cannot be lingered ~ the beauty and rawness of Australia cannot be levelled...!

*A land that is red, beautiful, and distant
and too far to travel by car...!*

*So, while this time spent is on Australian
soil, I thank God for this gift and the
opportunity to share,*

*the love of the country and the
experiences there...!*

*Australia and Christmas are unique and
of their own...*

*So, take the opportunity to enjoy and
refrain from the moan...!*

Photograph courtesy of Luke

Liz
Thank You

A young Aboriginal girl came to me for a job one day...

I employed her as she willing to learn...!

A few days later she arrived for her first day of work...

She fitted in well and showed great concern...

She was now independent and capable to earn...!

She showed willingness and adapted easily to the job...

One day, when the workroom was busy, and all hands were on deck, Liz announced proudly, 'I'm part of the mob...!'

From that moment on, her learning took on at great pace...

For Liz had a challenge and was part of the race...!

Her talents and skills grew at great speed...

And knew what to do without any heed...!

When it came to creativity, she could adapt and produce artwork of beauty to fit a customer's needs...

Liz quickly grew into the young woman she had intended to be...!

For life had its challenges for the time she had spent...

*She adapted her learning to the time
she'd been lent...!*

*Her determination beyond and
outstanding, her knowledge she gained...*

*She worked hard and was genuine
beyond belief,
for Liz had the journey for which she was
named...*

But as time was passing, Liz had a calling

To her people she knew ~

*A calling to be answered from many and
too few...!*

*It was now time for Liz to go on the
journey of starting anew...!*

A Time of Reflection ~ The Australian

A time of reflection is held by many when they come to live in this land of plenty...!

How lucky we are for this opportunity present,

for life in this country is there when you work hard, are wise and pleasant...!

For working hard and staying on goal, you're sure of the longing to find your prize and the opportunity present...!

Times can be tough even though you think, 'you have done all you can do...!'

That is the learning that will get you through...

You know from times spent, you have
given your best and it maybe just now,
you need to find time for a rest...!

A rest will help you recover for the effort
you've spent, and you know that the time
you have is the time that is lent...!

Life is for living and it's your challenge to
find ~ that opportunity out there which is
willing and kind...!

Your life's pathway is for walking and
seeing it through, and yet,
you may falter, but that is not what you
do...!

So be strong as you must, be creative,
work with your mind ~ for your mind is
your friend and the pathway you'll find...!

It's not always easy, but be sure to know,
that the gifts you deserve through the
work you have done...

Are waiting for you, just learn to have fun...!

For life is for living and you are in charge ~ if you give up now you will go on the run...!

This land of plenty is there for us all – but life has its prize and the way that you fall...!

It's now time to reflect on the pathway ahead, be positive and thoughtful and listen for the voice from within...

For within your own mind, you will hear your own voice call...!

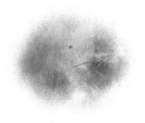

The Aussie Builder...

With utes and their Hi Vis[1] shirts,
the Aussie builders are a breed their
own...

Not forgetting the need for their mobile
phone...!

With all 'hands on deck', the Boss quickly
says, '...there's four thousand bricks to
lay today.... ~

there's simply no time to sleep in the
hay...!'

The Aussie builder is of one and takes
great delight to work in the sun...!

While he knows his brickies are out for
some fun...!

---

[1] *A Hi Vis is the bright iridescent yellow top all builders are, by law, required to wear.*

For time is a ticking and the building is right....!

'Just one hundred more bricks' he shouts, 'and we'll stop for the night...!'

To lay that number of bricks has been one hell of fight...!

With a day's work done, they head for the pub...

They need a beer to settle the dust...!

With the cold beer down, the Boss says out loud,

'Right boys, I'm heading home to the Mrs and straight for the tub...

...for you boys have done well today and makes a man proud for each Aussie builder stands out in the crowd...'

The Magpie's Calling

The magpie's song of early morning...

There's nothing so happy as it's calling...!

The magpie's song is an Australian treasure when all that is needed is the time to measure...!

Living abroad as someone must...

the magpie's calling makes the heart pause and gives this yearning for the pleasure...!

She hears the sound while phoning her friend and says, 'I hear the magpies calling...!'

And brings back the longing of that land while her heart is a falling....!

The magpie's calling is unique and yet,
for its own...!

With chorus, and choirs they fill the
sky...!

There's nothing as distinctive as the
sounds when in your bed you lie...!

Photograph courtesy Chris Stenger

Life
In The 21st Century

A Cup of Coffee!

'A Latte for you, A Cappuccino with skimmed and a Short Black...?' He asks...!

For the coffee you are a gasping...

For the caffeine is a grasping...!

The aroma passes your nose; your body is a shaking from your head to your toes...!

Your taste buds are anxious for the first sip and so it goes...!

In just a moment, your satisfaction will be heady...!

That coffee you're longing is just about ready...!

That time is so long as you keep yourself steady...!

And yes, he hands the drink and the first sip you take...!

That taste is so good, now your senses you make...!

With disposable cup in hand...

You stride the street ready and the symbol is seen...

The essence is great...

The caffeine 'hits' as you go...!

This cup of coffee is yours and you're out for the show...!

The caffeine is good; you are now as one...!

You can now cope with the problems given...

And those under the sun...!

Photograph courtesy Ekrulila

Age...

Age is a blessing and in disguise...

It shows a life lived where memories hide...

Times shared, and a reflection for some...!

Age is a time in life where challenges and thoughts are as one...!

The time to reflect and build on the knowledge once learned...!

Age can be timeless, and a lifetime you've earned...!

When you reflect on the stars or the sunshine above...!

*The raindrops and rivers and the
diamonds of light*

*are just there for you though you may
feel '...you've had one hell of a fight...!'*

The time is now and just for the living...!

*So now is the time for you to be thankful
and giving...!*

*Giving to you first is the start of a new
way of living...*

*For each day is of value and to be lived
moment by moment...*

*It's the moments that count, for within,
is the time that is freedom for you...!*

*For now, this richness of time is a
pleasure to see your life through...*

For within each moment you'll find, it's a great treasure to have...!

So, take this opportunity to re-start your life...

Think and do your dreams to fulfil...!

Regardless of what is said, you do as your will...!

Age is a gift and one to be cherished by all...

For within this time you have the power to show, that life is for living and sharing with love and, as you go, this is your call...!

Photograph courtesy
Edu Carvaho

How Hard They Work...!
For The Small Business Owner

Some work from dawn to dusk, working
and saving to make a crust...!

The small business owner is on their own
when it comes to making choices to make
ends meet...!

For everyday it's becoming more difficult
to compete...!

Sometimes, it's the wrong location for the
business they start...

Or is it that government policy has
changed and doesn't give a heart...!

For the small business owner, they are
out for the haul and cannot listen to the
voices that call:

'don't do that...!'

or

'make a new start...!'

The time is a testing the role they have chosen, but for many their financial state is quite frozen...!

The banks do not help when the time is so pressured...

For the business owner is financially measured...!

The bank manager looks at the figures he sees; the numbers in black and white featured he reads...!

And looks on again with great ease...! To see how the red numbers' show...!

The numbers don't reveal the effort now
sewn

~ only the numbers of interest related to
the overdraft or loan...!

Numbers that can make a bank manager
moan and become very mean...!

While he sits in his richly decked office
and there to be seen...!

He acts like the executioner there
while sitting in his large leather chair...!

The banks make more profit than a small
business owner can fare...

Small business owners are the largest
employers in Australia there...!

Without their support, the banks would
falter, and many a bank manager's head
would be out for the slaughter...!

So, with time on their side, the small business owner has the means to respond...!

To make their choices to the money system, right now and beyond...!

Scammers

Don't Let the Scammers Intimidate You

In this time, we live with internet usage and the information age...!

It gives scammers a unique and open stage...!

These people will try every tactic they can to gain your attention and get onto your page...!

They have no limitations for the manipulation they use,

From:

'You are my beloved...'
'You are like a sister to me...'
'I have been looking for you all my life...'
'I have a message for you...'
'You are always on my mind...!'

and now:

the Attached Invoice they send...!

All schemes are used to take money from you together to harm and offend...!

These people are constantly seeking and eager to find...

A person who's willing and extremely kind...!

Scammers have no limitations to the tricks they use...!

They entwine their malicious deeds into your heart to hurt and abuse...!

It's time to take action for this time is NOW...!

A scammer's plans can be hampered, and their deadly deeds stopped...

*By not paying attention they will surely
be flopped...!*

*Each and, every scammer has their own
intention at heart...!*

*You will make yourself a victim from the
actions you do and the emotions you feel
at the start...!*

*But now is the time to say, 'STOP,' with
your dignity intact and as part of the plot*

Act...

Which is now a known fact...!

*Do not again, reply or open the
Attachment*

For you which is meant...

Surely and abruptly,

Make this a new start and put all scamming messages promptly into the

Delete Cart...!

Minions...
For Those People Who Feel They Have No Purpose Other Than Earning Money

Their tasks are a daily grind when the only job available is of the minion kind...!

With little to no expression shown...

The minion is in a world of their own...!

With such systems in place, there is no permission to think...!

For one step out of line they can end in the drink...!

With a mortgage to pay, and children to raise, the process of living enters into a non-effective haze...!

The human mind is 'dumbed down' and frustration is felt...!

For many, this is too much, and a change is required...

When all that is needed is a word of kindness or their work admired...!

When said,

'That's a good job...'

Or

'Well done, it's great that you're here and giving a hand....'

Or

'Thank you, the deadline's met...'

A world of people are out there doing the jobs that don't fit and yet...

The need is too great to get up and quit...!

The minion is such, regardless of the way they feel...!

They are 'stuck' between the Cogs and the Wheel...!

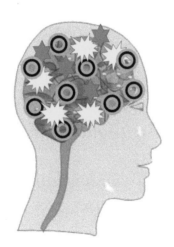

The Dishwasher!
For The Women Of Syria, With Love...

As we sit and watch the devastation on our TV's...

We become used to the sites as we feel the sea breeze...!

A woman dressed in traditional dress is bewildered as she sits on her lounge chair without any ease...!

I look, I see, from her lounge room to mine...

Her life is upheaval and mine is just fine...!

The camera pans in, and to the woman we see,

the shadows of pain are seen on her face...

Her lounge room is dusty, her curtains hang in great shreds...

The dishwasher, it's door is unfixed, and no longer can wash the dishes as before, and cannot be fixed...!

She looks exhausted from the pain and the war...

For all she wants is her life to restore...!

The GFC
We Don't Need Another GFC

In 2008 the GFC came and went...

For the governments bailed out the banks for the money they'd spent...!

Toxic mortgages caused the pain...

For greed was rampant and too hard for the banks to refrain...!

Without a care in the world, the loan agents had much to gain...

Responsibility was nil for the trouble caused...!

Many homes were lost, and many families were paused...!

*Their lives would not be the same again
for greed had overtaken...!*

The money system flawed...!

*So, credit may be good when we all act as
one, but the financial system is such,
when honesty is ignored...!*

*Another GFC will happen when bad deeds
are done...!*

*Because human nature is such, many
minds will have fun...!*

*So, be aware, when the banks are too big,
and opportunities present, greed will
take over and money is spent...*

*We, the individual need to make choices,
and that can be done...!*

*For banks that cause problems are no
good at all ~*

It's now up to us to make sure that governments do as we call...!

Drugs

Drugs are rampant as we know...!

*For the human brain is not made to take
~ this kind of abuse and the substance
they sew...!*

The brain is a delicate structure...

*The mind more so, than a person can
muster...!*

*Drugs don't forgive and the damage is
done...*

*And, sadly enough people think they are
out to have fun...!*

*If one is lucky, the journey back to
recovery can be done...!*

While the time is still yours, think twice
before you take the first one...!

Your life is at stake and the hurt you will
feel...!

For the simple action of the taking the
first pill...!

For your brain and mind are a gift to
you...

There to help you your whole life
through...!

With this said, drugs only make another
rich...!

So, make this time and the moment you
ditch...!

Say, 'No' with your mind and then with
your words...

Taking the first one is of no benefit at all...!

It's a road to destruction and will contribute to your downfall...!

The Human Brain
Getting To Know Your Brain

The human brain is far too important to ignore...

From the moment of birth, it's not mentioned, and seems to exist no more...!

For child education there's none in the store...!

For each adult living, and their child education had...

How important the brain is to live life and more...!

For adults will struggle to live the life they dream...

When the brain they have, is not understood or seen...!

Each person's brain is a treasure to have
but little is known, and people are not
very keen...!

A brain is a gift which needs to work ~
when a brain is idle the devilment is
seen...!

It's a bit of grey matter with neurons and
pathways shooting out sparks...!

And while you're asleep it works hard in
the dark...!

For now, is the time to take the time to
reflect...

To this treasure you have for if this is not
done you will live your life...

But with little effect and much regret...!

The Human Mind
Loving Your Human Mind

As research goes on...

The human mind is evasive and without any boundaries it's difficult to know...!

Just how far one's mind will stretch and grow...!

For within the minds we all have, are our dreams and our goals...!

But without understanding how these phenomenon roles...!

Great theorist and scholars have long asked questions...

And philosophy takes...

*The power of the mind and the choices
we make...!*

*For without an understanding, men
would not have walked on the moon...!*

*Nor would space exploration be now and
in the soon...!*

*And too, great medical advances as we
all know...!*

*None of this would be happening without
the minds we have and the power to
sew...!*

*For the human mind is always
enquiring...*

*Its mission is in the 'NOW' and in the
finding...!*

So, take the time to think of your mind...

Your mind holds secrets, yet to uncover...!

And is there to support you on the pathways you discover...!

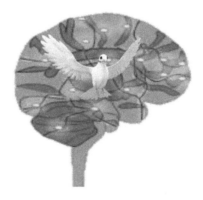

We Will Make The Difference –
The Coronavirus

The Coronavirus, a virus to detest
We now need solutions and vaccines are
the best...

Our scientists are working hard to
remedy the situation...

But we too, are responsible to stay within
our location...!

Governments are asking their words to
adhere...

By doing this, we will learn to manage
the fear...

To not comply, the situation is dire
And, we know, if we don't, our nation will
be within fire...!

The solution is not only with the scientists mentioned above...

But with us all and the people we love –

Let's do our bit to make our world a safe place –

To create a world where children learn and with a future to yearn...

As adults, we must make it happen, but it takes responsibility by us to earn...!

The responsibility is ours and ignore at our peril, for this virus contributes and belongs to the devil...!